W9-CKI-583

12 REASONS TO LOVE THE
BOSTON RED SOX

by Matt Tustison

STORY
LIBRARY

www.12StoryLibrary.com

12-Story Library is an imprint of Peterson Publishing Company and Press Room Editions.

Produced for 12-Story Library by Red Line Editorial

Photographs ©: Chris Szagola/AP Images, cover, 1; National Photo Company Collection/ Library of Congress, 5, 29; Sue Ogrocki/AP Images, 6; Winslow Townson/AP Images, 7, 16, 28; Joyce Vincent/Shutterstock Images, 8; Jason Tench/Shutterstock Images, 9; AP Images, 10; Peter J. Carroll/AP Images, 11; Richard Drew/AP Images, 13; Harry Cabluck/AP Images, 14; Jack Dempsey/AP Images, 17; Charlie Riedel/AP Images, 18, 24; Elise Amendola/ AP Images, 19; Kathy Willens/AP Images, 21; George Grantham Bain Collection/Library of Congress, 22; Chris Carlson/AP Images, 23; David J. Phillip/AP Images, 27

ISBN
978-1-63235-209-5 (hardcover)
978-1-63235-236-1 (paperback)
978-1-62143-261-6 (hosted ebook)

Library of Congress Control Number: 2015934314

Printed in the United States of America
Mankato, MN
October, 2015

Go beyond the book. Get free, up-to-date content on this topic at 12StoryLibrary.com.

TABLE OF CONTENTS

THE BABE'S LEGEND BEGINS IN BOSTON

George Herman "Babe" Ruth made his major league debut for the Red Sox on July 11, 1914. At first, Ruth was a pitcher for the Red Sox who occasionally batted as well. And he was quite a pitcher. Ruth was a key member of the Red Sox's 1916 World Series team. But soon he started to get attention for his hitting, too.

In 1918, he pitched less and began playing in the outfield. Doing so allowed him to be in the everyday lineup. This was in the so-called "dead-ball era." Not many home runs were hit. Still, Ruth led the American League (AL) with 11 home runs. The Red Sox won the World Series again. Ruth earned two victories on the mound in the Series.

By 1919, Ruth played even more in the outfield. The left-handed hitter

THE CURSE OF THE BAMBINO

The Red Sox were one of baseball's best teams in the early 1900s. They won five World Series through the 1919 season. Then they sold Babe Ruth to the New York Yankees. Soon after, the Yankees began a run. They won 26 World Series between then and 2003. The Red Sox, meanwhile, won none. It was "The Curse of the Bambino."

belted a then-major-league record 29 home runs. Ruth asked for a salary increase. But Red Sox owner Harry Frazee decided instead to sell his

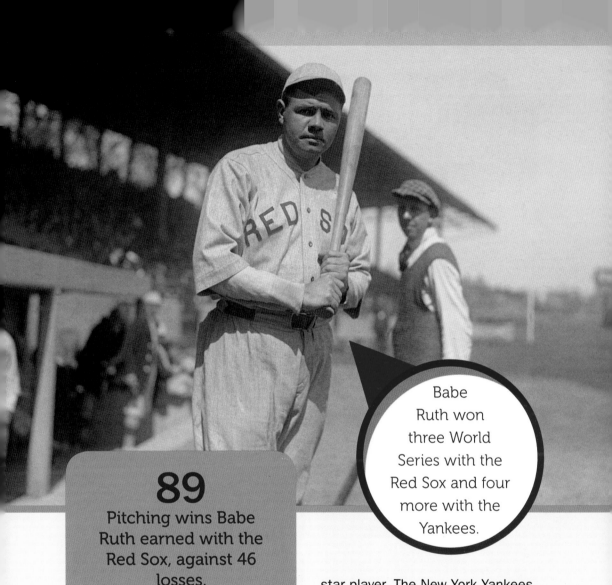

89

Pitching wins Babe Ruth earned with the Red Sox, against 46 losses.

- He had an earned-run average (ERA) of 2.19 with Boston.
- Ruth won two of his 12 AL home run titles while in Boston.
- When he retired, Ruth held the single-season (60 in 1927) and career (714) records for home runs.

star player. The New York Yankees agreed to pay more than $100,000 for the player nicknamed "The Bambino."

Ruth's big swing would result in even more home runs with the Yankees. He led them to four World Series titles. For the Red Sox, Ruth's departure began "The Curse of the Bambino."

THE CURSE ENDS: 2004 SOX WIN IT ALL

It looked as if "The Curse of the Bambino" would continue in 2004. The Red Sox met the New York Yankees in that year's AL playoffs. The winner would go to the World Series. But the Yankees won the first three games. They needed just one more.

Game 4 was in Boston. The Yankees led 4–3 going into the bottom of the ninth. Superstar closer Mariano Rivera came in to close out the game. But pinch runner Dave Roberts stole second base. Then Bill Mueller drove him in to tie the game. Later, in the bottom of the 12th, David Ortiz's two-run homer gave Boston a 6–4 win.

Ortiz had the game-winning hit in Game 5, too. His single gave the Red Sox

The Red Sox celebrate after beating the Cardinals to win the 2004 World Series.

Red Sox pitcher Curt Schilling pitched against the Yankees in Game 6 despite having three stitches in his injured ankle. With blood on his sock, he led Boston to a 4–2 win.

0

Major league teams that came back to win a playoff series after losing the first three games—until the Red Sox did it in 2004.

- The 2004 Red Sox finished 98–64 and second in the AL East.
- Boston qualified for the playoffs as the AL wild-card team.
- Manny Ramirez was named World Series Most Valuable Player (MVP).

a 5–4 win in 14 innings. Then the Red Sox won Game 6 and Game 7, too. With the Yankees out of the way, the World Series was a breeze. Boston swept the St. Louis Cardinals in four games. For the first time since 1918, the Red Sox were World Series champs. The curse was over.

"I'm so proud of being a part of the greatest Red Sox team in history," pitcher Curt Schilling said.

FENWAY PARK: HOME FOR OVER 100 YEARS

There's no place quite like Fenway Park. The Red Sox's home stadium opened in 1912. That makes it the oldest ballpark in the major leagues.

The most famous feature of Fenway Park is the Green Monster. The Monster is a green left-field wall that is more than 37 feet (11 m) high. The fence stretches 231 feet (70 m) across. The wall was originally blue. It also featured many advertisements. In 1947, the ads were scraped off. Meanwhile, the wall was painted green to match the rest of Fenway Park.

The Monster sits 310 feet (94 m) from home plate. This is the shortest distance for a left-field fence in the majors. Fenway Park also has the shortest distance to a right-field fence—302 feet (92 m) at the foul pole. That pole is

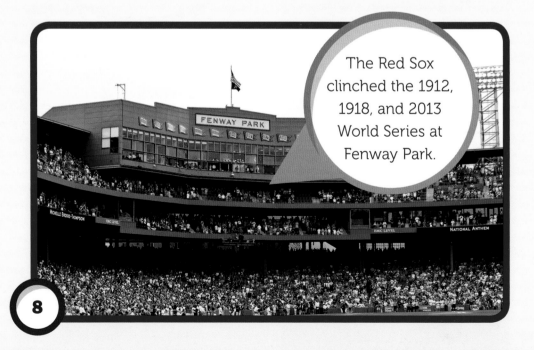

The Red Sox clinched the 1912, 1918, and 2013 World Series at Fenway Park.

Fenway Park's famous Green Monster

820

Consecutive games, including the playoffs, with sellout crowds at Fenway Park from 2003 to 2013. This is a major-league record.

- Fenway Park was built in 1912 and rebuilt in 1934.
- Many other events have been held there, including football games and hockey's Winter Classic.
- All of the seats are green except one. A red seat marks the longest home run ever hit in the stadium (by Ted Williams in 1946).

nicknamed "Pesky's Pole" in honor of Johnny Pesky. He was a Red Sox infielder in the 1940s and 1950s. As legend had it, some of his six career home runs at Fenway were hit just inside the pole.

THINK ABOUT IT

Fenway Park is more than 100 years old. Do you think the Red Sox should build a new ballpark like other teams? List five reasons to support your answer.

TEDDY BALLGAME MAKES HITTING HIS EXPERTISE

Many baseball historians say Ted Williams was the greatest hitter who ever lived. The Red Sox left fielder had a picture-perfect left-handed stroke. His swing was developed through endless hours of practice.

Ted Williams swings through on his 500th home run in a 1960 game against the Cleveland Indians.

"Teddy Ballgame" broke into the majors with the Red Sox at age 20 in 1939. He became an immediate star. And he would only get better. His career batting average of .344 is tied for the seventh-best in baseball history. It is the highest average of anyone who played his entire career after 1920.

In 1941, Williams had a legendary season. He finished with a .406 batting average. He is the last player in the majors to hit .400.

.388

Ted Williams's batting average in 1957 at age 39. He became the oldest player to win a league batting title.

- Williams won six AL batting titles in his career.
- He was the AL MVP in 1946 and 1949.
- Williams was inducted into the Baseball Hall of Fame in 1966.

"Some call it courage," Williams once said of his approach to hitting. "I call it confidence in yourself. Knowing you can hit any pitcher alive."

TIME IN THE MILITARY

Ted Williams's time in the major leagues was twice interrupted by his service in the US military. He spent 1943 to 1945 with the navy in World War II. Later he flew combat missions for the marines in the Korean War. That caused him to miss most of the 1952 and 1953 seasons.

Williams helped the Red Sox reach the 1946 World Series against the St. Louis Cardinals. But they lost in seven games. Williams ended his career with 521 home runs. He hit a dramatic homer in his last at-bat in 1960 in front of the home crowd at Fenway Park.

Ted Williams doubles against the New York Yankees in a 1958 game.

YAZ PICKS UP WHERE WILLIAMS LEFT OFF

When Carl Yastrzemski was growing up, he helped his father on the family potato farm. After school, he would lift the heavy 75-pound (34 kg) potato sacks onto the tractor carts. He would say to himself, "This is going to make me strong, help me make it to the big leagues."

His dream came true in 1961 with the Red Sox. "Yaz" had very big shoes to fill in left field. He was replacing Ted Williams. The Red Sox's legend had retired after the previous season.

Yaz was ready for the challenge. He won seven Gold Glove awards for his outstanding defense. He also became an excellent hitter. Yaz won three AL batting championships with his left-handed swing.

In 1967, Yastrzemski had a spectacular year. He won the AL Triple Crown. That meant he led the league in hitting (.326 batting average), home runs (44), and runs batted in (RBIs) (121). This feat would not be matched again until 2012.

The 1967 Red Sox captured the AL pennant on the last day of the season. Yastrzemski shined in the World Series. He hit .400 with three home runs against the St. Louis Cardinals. But the Red Sox fell in seven games.

THINK ABOUT IT

Why do you think it's so rare for a player to win the Triple Crown? What are some of the skills a player must have to excel in all three statistics?

Yastrzemski retired after the 1983 season. He finished his career with 3,419 hits and 452 home runs. Through 2014, Yaz was one of just eight big league players to have at least 3,000 hits and 400 homers.

3,419

Carl Yastrzemski's career hits. That ranked ninth on baseball's all-time list through 2014.

- Yaz was an 18-time All-Star.
- He won the 1967 AL MVP Award.
- He was inducted into the Baseball Hall of Fame in 1989.

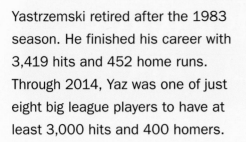

The Red Sox's Carl Yastrzemski blasts a home run against the New York Yankees in 1980.

CARLTON FISK WAVES THE BALL FAIR

Game 6 of the 1975 World Series was at Fenway Park. It was a must-win for the Red Sox. They were down three games to two against the Cincinnati Reds. A loss would end Boston's season.

Boston's Carlton Fisk wills his hit to stay fair in Game 6 of the 1975 World Series.

4

Different decades in which Carlton Fisk played in the major leagues.

- He made his debut in 1969 and played his last game in 1993.
- Fisk played for the Red Sox (1969, 1971–1980) and Chicago White Sox (1981–1993).
- He was named to 11 All-Star Games over his career.

WEARING A RED SOX CAP AT THE HALL

Carlton Fisk played 11 seasons with the Red Sox. Then he played 13 more with the Chicago White Sox. Over his career, he caught 2,226 games. That ranked second in baseball history through 2014. In 2000, he was inducted into the Baseball Hall of Fame. After much thought, he chose a Red Sox hat for his plaque. "I think this has always been a part of me," Fisk said.

Neither team let up. The game headed into extra innings with the score tied at 6–6. And it was still going at 12:30 a.m. Catcher Carlton "Pudge" Fisk led off for the Red Sox in the bottom of the 12th inning. On the second pitch, he lofted a high shot down the left-field line.

Fisk took off for first base as the ball sailed toward the Green Monster. As he ran, he waved wildly, willing the ball to stay fair. The ball hit the foul pole. That meant it was a fair ball. Home run! The Red Sox would live another day.

"I knew it had the distance and the height," recalled Fisk, who grew up in nearby New Hampshire. "I just wasn't sure it was going to stay fair."

The Red Sox lost 4–3 in Game 7. But Fisk had provided an all-time classic World Series moment.

15

SOX CELEBRATE ANOTHER TITLE IN 2007

"The Curse of the Bambino" haunted the Red Sox for 86 years. They finally broke the streak with a World Series win in 2004. The wait for their next title wasn't nearly as long.

In 2007, Red Sox topped the New York Yankees for the AL East title. Then they overcame the Cleveland Indians in the AL Championship Series (ALCS). It wasn't easy. Cleveland had a 3–1 series lead. But Red Sox pitcher Josh Beckett allowed just one run in eight innings in Game 5. Boston won 7–1. Then the Red Sox coasted to wins in the next two games, too.

Kevin Youkilis slides in to score for the Red Sox in Game 1 of the 2007 World Series.

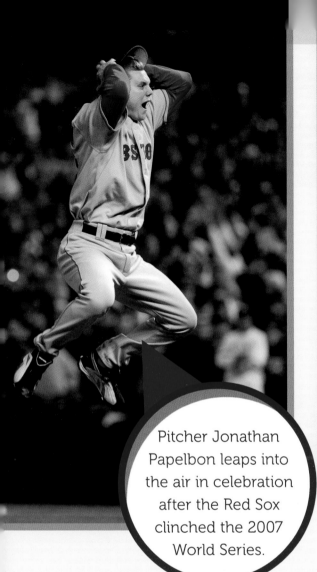

1.20

Josh Beckett's ERA in the 2007 playoffs. He had a 4–0 record.

- Boston finished the regular season with a 96–66 record and won the AL East.
- The Red Sox ended the Yankees' run of nine straight division crowns.
- David Ortiz led the Red Sox with a .332 batting average and 35 home runs.
- Beckett led Boston with a 20–7 record and 3.27 ERA.

Pitcher Jonathan Papelbon leaps into the air in celebration after the Red Sox clinched the 2007 World Series.

"We worked too hard all year," said rookie second baseman Dustin Pedroia, who homered and drove in five runs in Game 7. "Nobody wanted to go home."

After the ALCS, the World Series was a breeze. The Red Sox coasted to four wins in a row over the Colorado Rockies. Boston left-hander Jon Lester picked up the World Series-clinching victory in his first postseason start. Mike Lowell homered and earned series MVP honors. Boston had to wait 86 years for its sixth World Series. The seventh came just three years later.

"It doesn't get old," manager Terry Francona said.

RED SOX ARE BOSTON STRONG IN 2013

The Red Sox had to wait 86 years for the 2004 World Series win. They had to wait even longer for a World Series win at Fenway Park. The last time that had happened was in 1918. Few expected that drought to end in 2013, though.

The Red Sox had been miserable in 2012. They finished last in the AL East. But they turned it around quickly. Boston won 97 games and the division title. Then the Red Sox got back to the World Series. And after five games, they led the St. Louis Cardinals three games to two.

Game 6 was in Boston. Fenway Park was jammed with 38,447 singing, shouting fans. When Koji Uehara struck out Matt Carpenter for the final out, the celebration was on. Players danced around the infield with their families. Fans remained in the stands to savor the moment.

"Maybe they won't have to go another 95 years," said John Farrell, a champion in his first season as Boston's manager.

Boston's Jonny Gomes celebrates after hitting a home run in Game 4 of the 2013 World Series.

The "Boston Strong" logo was designed into the field at Fenway Park during the 2013 playoffs.

BOSTON STRONG

The 2013 Red Sox were playing for a city shaken by tragedy. Terrorists had set off bombs the previous April at the world-famous Boston Marathon. Three people died. More than 260 were wounded. Bostonians stood together. They called themselves "Boston Strong." The Red Sox wore "Boston Strong" logos on their left sleeves. They also placed an emblem on the center-field grass as a constant reminder.

1

Pitchers to start and win a World Series-clinching game for more than one team. John Lackey did so for the Angels in 2002 and the Red Sox in 2014.

- Boston's 97–65 record was the best in AL East.
- David Ortiz was named the World Series MVP.
- Ortiz batted .688 with 11 hits, two home runs, and six RBIs in six games.

19

9

RED SOX AND YANKEES DUKE IT OUT FOR DECADES

Boston and New York are only approximately 200 miles (322 km) apart. The Red Sox and Yankees are natural rivals. The Yankees' lopsided success after "The Curse of the Bambino" made the rivalry even more heated.

The teams played many memorable games over the years. One was in 1978. The Red Sox had held a commanding eight-game lead in the AL East on July 20. The Yankees were 14 games back. But the Yankees surged, and the Red Sox slowed. The season ended with the teams tied. This forced a one-game playoff on October 2 at Fenway Park. New York won 5–4. The Yankees' Bucky Dent belted a three-run homer over the Green Monster. Dent only hit 40 homers in his 12-year career.

The Yankees crushed the Red Sox's spirit again in 2003. The teams met in that year's ALCS. New York won the series when Aaron Boone homered in the 11th inning of Game 7 at Yankee Stadium.

3

World Series wins for the Red Sox between 2004 and 2014.

- The Yankees won only one championship during that time.
- Through 2014, the Yankees had 27 World Series titles to the Red Sox's eight.
- The Yankees have had 40 hall of fame players while the Red Sox had 36.

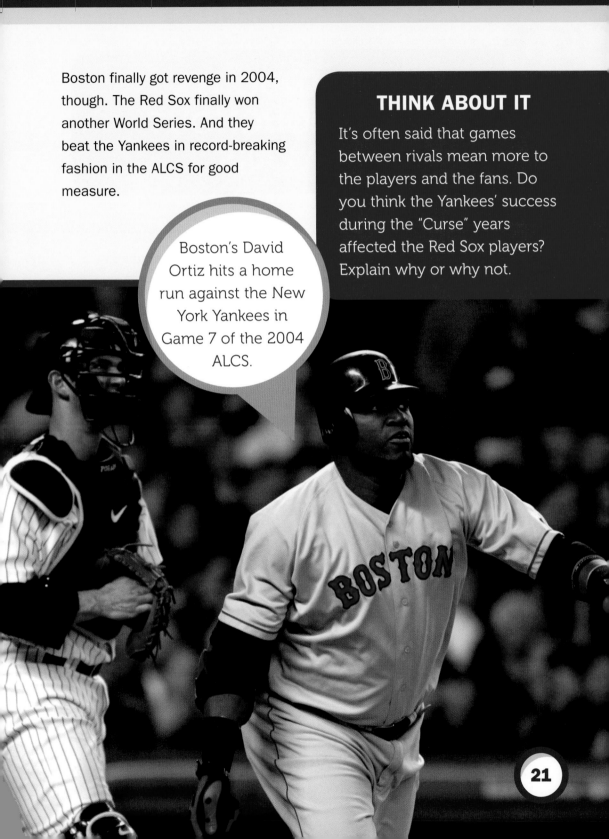

Boston finally got revenge in 2004, though. The Red Sox finally won another World Series. And they beat the Yankees in record-breaking fashion in the ALCS for good measure.

Boston's David Ortiz hits a home run against the New York Yankees in Game 7 of the 2004 ALCS.

THINK ABOUT IT

It's often said that games between rivals mean more to the players and the fans. Do you think the Yankees' success during the "Curse" years affected the Red Sox players? Explain why or why not.

SOX STANDOUTS STAR THROUGHOUT THE YEARS

Babe Ruth. Ted Williams. Carl Yastrzemski. Carlton Fisk. The Red Sox have had no shortage of star players throughout the years.

Cy Young in 1908

Cy Young set the standard for pitchers. He won a record 511 games. Of those wins, 192 came when he pitched for the Red Sox from 1901 to 1908. Roger Clemens later tied Young's team record. "The Rocket" played for Boston from 1984 to 1996. He won three AL Cy Young Awards during that time. Of course, that award is named after the former Red Sox star.

Pedro Martinez continued the great pitching tradition. The right-hander went 117–37 with Boston from 1998 to 2004.

He won back-to-back Cy Young Awards in 1999 and 2000.

Plenty of hitters shined in Boston, too. Center fielder Tris Speaker played in Boston from 1907 to 1915. He hit .337 during that time. First baseman Jimmie Foxx averaged 36 homers and 129 RBIs in his first six years with Boston, from 1936 to 1941. Left fielders Jim Rice (1974–1989) and Manny Ramirez (2001–2008) hit for average and power.

Hall of fame third baseman Wade Boggs had a left-handed swing tailor-made for Fenway Park. Boggs won five batting titles with Boston from 1982 to 1992.

And then there's David Ortiz. The designated hitter joined the Red Sox in 2003. His powerful home runs helped the team win a World Series one year later.

Pedro Martinez pitches in a 2004 game.

.691

The winning percentage for the 1912 Red Sox (105–47 record). It remains the highest in team history through 2014.

- Carl Yastrzemski leads the Red Sox in career hits with 3,419.
- Ted Williams leads the Red Sox in career home runs with 521.
- Cy Young and Roger Clemens are tied for the team lead in career wins with 192 each.
- Clemens leads the team with 2,590 career strikeouts.

23

RED SOX NATION STANDS TALL

The Red Sox played the New York Mets in the 1986 World Series. A newspaper reporter noted many fans from Connecticut cheered on the Red Sox. He called the fans "Red Sox Nation."

The tradition grew from there. In 2004, the Red Sox began to offer official membership in the Red Sox Nation. Each member gets a special membership card.

Fans celebrate atop the Green Monster after the Red Sox won the 2013 World Series.

"SWEET CAROLINE"

Singer Neil Diamond wrote "Sweet Caroline" in 1969. The song has been played at Fenway Park since at least 1997. Since 2002, it has been played in the middle of the eighth inning. The song has nothing to do with Boston, the Red Sox, or baseball. Yet it's become a cherished tradition at Fenway Park.

In 2007, members had an opportunity to run for president of Red Sox Nation. Candidates were narrowed to six finalists in a primary election. Journalist Tim Russert of NBC even moderated a debate among the finalists. Jerry Remy, a former Red Sox player, eventually won after an online election.

After his election, Remy called for the creation of governors. They each represent Red Sox Nation in their home states. Representatives were soon named for Massachusetts, Connecticut, Maine, New Hampshire, Rhode Island, and Vermont. Other states were added later.

37,673
Fenway Park's capacity. Only three major league ballparks seat fewer fans.

- *Forbes* magazine rated Red Sox Nation as best fans in American sports in 2010.
- Celebrity Red Sox fans include actors Ben Affleck, Matt Damon, and brothers Donnie and Mark Wahlberg.

THINK ABOUT IT

What makes a good fan? How should a fan react when his or her team is performing poorly? Explain your reasoning in a written paragraph. Use examples to make your case.

12

BIG PAPI COMES THROUGH IN THE CLUTCH

David Ortiz wasn't always a power-hitting superstar. In fact, the Minnesota Twins once released Ortiz. They soon regretted it. Ortiz signed with the Red Sox in 2003. The Dominican player then became one of baseball's most feared sluggers.

As a designated hitter, Ortiz rarely played in the field. He didn't have to. Ortiz drove in lots of runs. Many came off home runs. And many of Ortiz's hits came in clutch situations.

Ortiz played a big role on the Red Sox's 2004, 2007, and 2013 championship teams. Ortiz had two game-winning hits in the 2004 ALCS. He batted .370 with three home runs and 10 RBIs in the 2007 postseason. The best performance came in 2013.

OFF-THE-FIELD STAR, TOO

The David Ortiz Children's Fund was founded in 2005. The foundation raises funds and provides heart surgeries for children in the Dominican Republic and the United States. In 2011, Ortiz was presented with the Roberto Clemente Award. It is given each year to a player who is a star on the field and in the community.

Ortiz homered in Games 1 and 2 of the World Series. He ended with six RBIs and a remarkable .688 batting average. It was no surprise when he was named World Series MVP.

On August 16, 2014, Ortiz hit his 400th and 401st home runs as a

26

54

Home runs for David
Ortiz in 2006, a Red Sox
record.

- Ortiz led the AL in
  home runs that season.
- He twice led the league
  in RBIs (2005 and 2006).
- Ortiz's nickname is "Big
  Papi."

member of the Red Sox. He became
the third player to reach 400 with
Boston. Only Ted Williams (521) and
Carl Yastrzemski (452) had reached
that milestone.

David Ortiz blasts
a two-run home
run in the 2013
World Series.

12 KEY DATES

1901

The Boston Americans play their first season in the AL. The Americans, who won the 1903 World Series, would change their name to the Red Sox after the 1907 season.

1912

Fenway Park opens on April 20 in Boston. At the end of the season, the team, now known as the Red Sox, beats the New York Giants in the World Series.

1915

The Red Sox defeat the Philadelphia Phillies in the World Series. They defend their title the next year, beating the Brooklyn Robins.

1918

The Red Sox win the World Series against the Chicago Cubs. Babe Ruth earns two pitching victories for Boston, including a Game 1 shutout.

1920

The Red Sox sell Ruth to the New York Yankees, beginning "The Curse of the Bambino."

1941

The Red Sox's Ted Williams finishes the season with a .406 batting average. No player in baseball has hit .400 since.

1967

The Red Sox win the AL pennant in the "Impossible Dream" season. Boston then loses to St. Louis in seven games in the World Series.

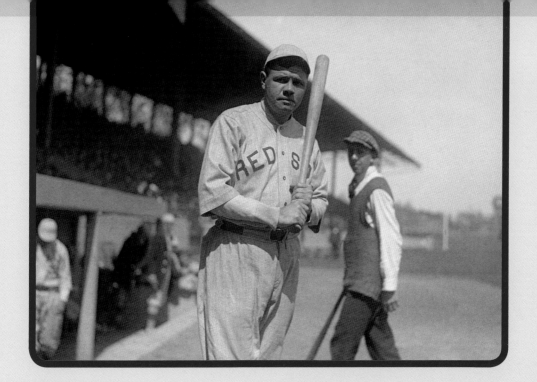

1975

Carlton Fisk hits a 12th-inning home run off the left-field foul pole, giving Boston a dramatic Game 6 victory over Cincinnati in the World Series. The Red Sox would lose Game 7.

1986

Roger Clemens strikes out a record 20 batters in a 3–1 win over the Seattle Mariners on April 29 (he matches the feat again in 1996). Boston rallies past the California Angels in the ALCS but falls to the New York Mets in the World Series.

2004

The Red Sox rally to beat the Yankees in the ALCS. They then sweep the Cardinals to win their first World Series in 86 years, ending "The Curse of the Bambino."

2007

Boston wins a second World Series in four seasons, sweeping the Colorado Rockies.

2013

The Red Sox defeat the Cardinals in Game 6 of the World Series on October 30, clinching their first title at Fenway Park since 1918.

GLOSSARY

clutch
In a very important or critical situation, especially during a sports competition.

curse
A cause of trouble or bad luck.

legendary
Well known and admired over a long period.

pennant
A league championship.

postseason
Games at the end of the season that decide a champion. When a team loses in the postseason, its season is over.

retire
To end one's baseball career, usually because of age.

rivalry
A state or situation in which people or groups of people are competing against one another.

rookie
A professional baseball player in his first year.

salary
The amount of money someone is paid to do a job.

wild-card
Playoff spots that go to the best teams that did not win their divisions.

FOR MORE INFORMATION

Books

The Boston Globe, and Larry Lucchino. *For Boston: From Worst to First, the Improbable Dream Season of the 2013 Red Sox*. Chicago: Triumph Books, 2013.

Bradlee Jr., Ben. *The Kid: The Immortal Life of Ted Williams*. New York: Back Bay Books, 2014.

Cohen, Robert W. *The 50 Greatest Players in Boston Red Sox History*. Rockport, ME: Down East Books, 2014.

Editors of Sports Illustrated. *Sports Illustrated Baseball's Greatest*. New York: Sports Illustrated, 2013.

Websites

Baseball-Reference
www.baseball-reference.com

Boston Red Sox
boston.redsox.mlb.com

Major League Baseball
www.mlb.com

INDEX

About the Author

Matt Tustison is a sports copyeditor at the *Washington Post*. He has also worked as a sports copyeditor at other newspapers, including the *St. Paul Pioneer Press*, and as an editor and writer of children's sports books at Red Line Editorial in Burnsville, Minnesota.

READ MORE FROM 12-STORY LIBRARY

Every 12-Story Library book is available in many formats, including Amazon Kindle and Apple iBooks. For more information, visit your device's store or 12StoryLibrary.com.

W9-CKI-575

HEPHAESTUS

God of Fire, Metalwork, and Building

BY TERI TEMPLE

ILLUSTRATED BY ROBERT SQUIER

Published by The Child's World®
1980 Lookout Drive • Mankato, MN 56003-1705
800-599-READ • www.childsworld.com

Acknowledgments
The Child's World®: Mary Berendes, Publishing Director
The Design Lab: Design and production
Red Line Editorial: Editorial direction

Design elements: Maksym Dragunov/Dreamstime;
Dreamstime

Photographs ©: Shutterstock Images, 5, 16; Panos
Karapanagiotis/Shutterstock Images, 10; Lefteris
Papaulakis/Shutterstock Images, 12; Catalin Voicu/
Shutterstock Images, 14; Stasys Eidiejus/Shutterstock
Images, 18; Marie-Lan Nguyen, 22; Uleanov/Shutterstock
Images, 28

ISBN 9781614732600
LCCN 2012932422

Printed in the United States of America
Mankato, MN
October 2013
PA02204

CONTENTS

INTRODUCTION

Long ago in ancient Greece and Rome, most people believed that gods and goddesses ruled their world. Storytellers shared the adventures of these gods to help explain all the mysteries in life. The gods were immortal, meaning they lived forever. Their stories were full of love and tragedy, fearsome monsters, brave heroes, and struggles for power. The storytellers wove aspects of Greek customs and beliefs into the tales. Some stories told of the creation of the world and the origins of the gods. Others helped explain natural events such as earthquakes and storms. People believed the tales, which over time became myths.

The ancient Greeks and Romans worshiped the gods by building temples and statues in their honor. They felt the gods would protect and guide them. People passed down the myths through the generations by word of mouth. Later, famous poets such as Homer and Hesiod wrote them down. Today, these myths give us a unique look at what life was like in ancient Greece more than 2,000 years ago.

ANCIENT GREEK SOCIETIES

IN ANCIENT GREECE, CITIES, TOWNS, AND THEIR SURROUNDING FARMLANDS WERE CALLED CITY-STATES. THESE CITY-STATES EACH HAD THEIR OWN GOVERNMENTS. THEY MADE THEIR OWN LAWS. THE INDIVIDUAL CITY-STATES WERE VERY INDEPENDENT. THEY NEVER JOINED TO BECOME ONE WHOLE NATION. THEY DID, HOWEVER, SHARE A COMMON LANGUAGE, RELIGION, AND CULTURE.

MOUNT OLYMPUS
The mountaintop home of the 12 Olympic gods

Aegean Sea

CRETE

APHRODITE (af-roh-DY-tee)
Goddess of love and beauty; born of the sea foam; wife of Hephaestus; mother of Eros

ARES (AIR-eez)
God of war; son of Zeus and Hera; possible father of Eros

ATHENA (a-THEE-na)
Goddess of wisdom; daughter of Zeus

CYCLOPES (SIGH-clopes)
One-eyed giants; children of Gaea and Uranus

HARMONIA
(hahr-MOH-nee-uh)
Daughter of Ares and Aphrodite; wife of Cadmus

ANCIENT GREECE

MOUNT ETNA
An active volcano in Sicily; underneath it was the workshop of Hephaestus

OLYMPIAN GODS
Demeter, Hermes, Hephaestus, Aphrodite, Ares, Hera, Zeus, Poseidon, Athena, Apollo, Artemis, and Dionysus

TROJAN WAR
War between the ancient Greeks and Trojans

TITANS (TIE-tinz)
The 12 children of Gaea and Cronus; godlike giants that are said to represent the forces of nature

HEPHAESTUS (huh-FES-tuhs)
God of fire, metalwork, and building; son of Zeus and Hera; married to Aphrodite

HERA (HEER-uh)
Queen of the gods; married to Zeus

MOMUS (MOH-muhs)
God of ridicule; judged a contest of the gods

PANDORA (pan-DAWR-uh)
First woman on Earth; created by Hephaestus; opened the box of evils out of curiosity

THETIS (THEE-tis)
Daughter of a sea nymph; mother of Greek hero Achilles; helped raise Hephaestus

ZEUS (ZOOS)
Supreme ruler of the heavens and weather and of the gods who lived on Mount Olympus; youngest son of Cronus and Rhea; married to Hera; father of many gods and heroes

Hephaestus was the mighty god of fire. He was also the best blacksmith and craftsman in the universe. Yet Hephaestus did not have a noble start in life. There are two versions of how Hephaestus came into the world. Hephaestus was the second son of Zeus and Hera, the king and queen of the Olympic gods. Ares, the god of war, was their first son. Hephaestus was as gentle as his brother Ares was cruel. The brothers lived with their parents high atop Mount Olympus. Zeus and Hera ruled the universe with their siblings Poseidon, Hades, Demeter, and Hestia.

In one version of Hephaestus's story, he was born as a perfect god like all the other gods. One day he tried to protect his mother from being punished by Zeus. This made Zeus furious. So Zeus took Hephaestus by the foot and hurled him from the heavens. Hephaestus fell all the way to Earth. His landing was abrupt and violent. It left Hephaestus disabled. Hephaestus returned to Mount Olympus humbled and unable to walk well. There the other gods laughed behind his back. It was a rocky start for the god of fire.

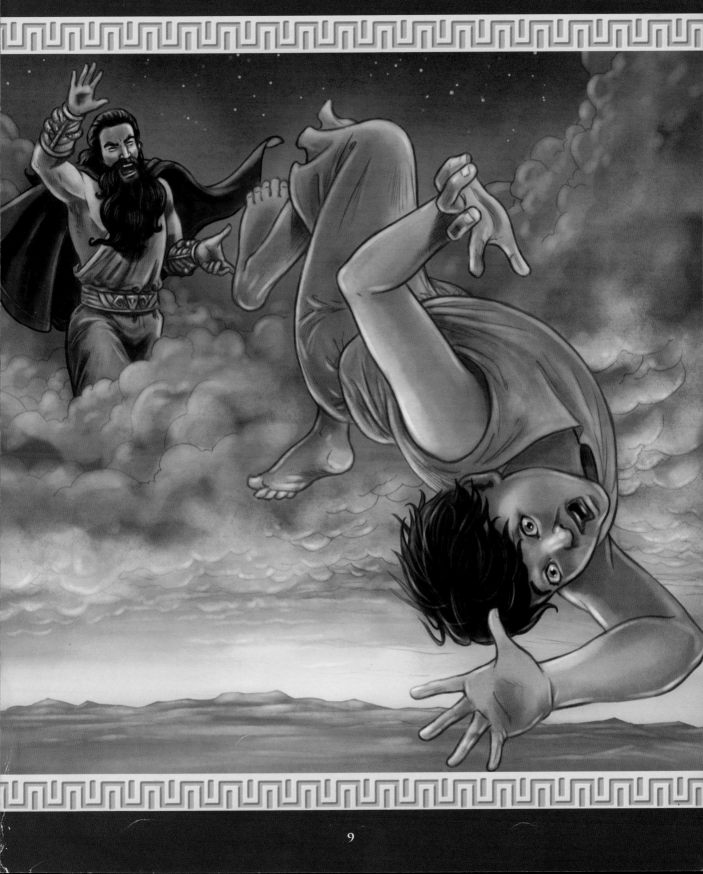

THETIS AND ACHILLES

THETIS HELPED RAISE HEPHAESTUS, BUT SHE ALSO
HAD A SON NAMED ACHILLES. SHE WANTED TO
MAKE ACHILLES IMMORTAL LIKE THE GODS.
THETIS KNEW THE RIVER STYX IN
THE UNDERWORLD HAD MAGICAL

The second version of Hephaestus's story is not much happier. Hera was angry with Zeus for having his daughter Athena, who sprang from his forehead. So she decided to have a child all on her own. Hera became pregnant by the sheer force of her will. When her son Hephaestus was born, Hera's joy turned to disgust. Hephaestus had been born with a clubbed foot and would be lame. A lame person has difficulty walking because of an injury to the foot or leg. Hephaestus was also ugly. Hera threw him right off Mount Olympus.

Hephaestus fell for nine days and nights before landing in the ocean. Two sea nymphs found him near the island of Lemnos. The sea nymphs, Thetis and Eurynome, rescued Hephaestus. They took him to their underwater cave. Together they raised him for the first nine years of his life. Hephaestus began to learn his craft in the secret cave. He collected pearls and jewels from the ocean floor. Then Hephaestus made them into beautiful pieces of jewelry.

PROPERTIES. SO THETIS HELD ACHILLES BY THE HEEL AND DIPPED HIM IN THE RIVER. THE PARTS OF HIS BODY THAT TOUCHED THE RIVER BECAME VERY STRONG. ACHILLES HAD JUST ONE WEAK SPOT—THE HEEL WHERE HIS MOTHER HELD HIM. IT WOULD BE HIS UNDOING. ACHILLES WAS KILLED DURING THE TROJAN WAR WHEN AN ARROW PIERCED HIS HEEL. TODAY THE EXPRESSION "ACHILLES'S HEEL" REFERS TO A PERSON'S WEAKNESS.

Hephaestus grew up to be the god of fire, craftsmen, and metalworkers. He was very fond of artists and sculptors. Hephaestus was also the blacksmith of the gods. In ancient Greece many blacksmiths were lame. This disability made it so they could no longer work as warriors, hunters, or farmers. Hephaestus became the god with a special interest in helping the lame.

The other gods admired Hephaestus for his skills as a craftsman. As the only working god, Hephaestus was strong and full of life. His work at the blacksmith's forge gave him a thick neck and heavily muscled arms. Hephaestus was often shown as a fully bearded middle-aged man. Hephaestus was hairy and constantly sweaty, which did not add to his charm. Despite his ugly appearance Hephaestus was a gentle and peace-loving god. He was the opposite of his fiery brother Ares. These two siblings would become rivals.

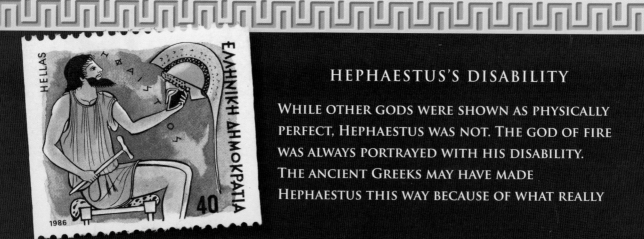

HEPHAESTUS'S DISABILITY

WHILE OTHER GODS WERE SHOWN AS PHYSICALLY PERFECT, HEPHAESTUS WAS NOT. THE GOD OF FIRE WAS ALWAYS PORTRAYED WITH HIS DISABILITY. THE ANCIENT GREEKS MAY HAVE MADE HEPHAESTUS THIS WAY BECAUSE OF WHAT REALLY

HAPPENED TO BLACKSMITHS IN ANCIENT TIMES. BLACKSMITHS WERE OFTEN
POISONED BY THEIR WORK. BLACKSMITHS ADDED ARSENIC TO THE BRONZE
THEY USED. ARSENIC IS A POISON. ARSENIC POISONING OFTEN RESULTS IN
LAMENESS. HEPHAESTUS DID NOT LET HIS DISABILITY SLOW HIM DOWN. HE IS
OFTEN CREDITED WITH INVENTING THE FIRST WHEELCHAIR.

ANCIENT GREEK CRAFTSMEN

Shops in ancient Greece were often small and family run. Family members worked with a few slaves. What the individual craftsmen made

14

One of Hephaestus's first jobs was to build the palace for the gods on Mount Olympus. He used gold and metals of every color to create beautiful designs all over the palace. He is considered by many to be the father of invention. Hephaestus first had to create the tools he needed. He made hammers, tongs, and anvils. Hephaestus even built robots of gold and silver to help him in his workshop.

Hephaestus was not just talented. He was generous as well. He created thrones, beautiful jewelry, chariots, and strong weapons for his fellow Olympic gods. For Hermes he made winged sandals and a messenger hat. Zeus requested a breastplate from Hephaestus, called the Aegis. Hephaestus even fastened the head of the Gorgon Medusa to it to make it more powerful. One look at the snake-haired Gorgon could turn a person to stone. For Achilles and Heracles, Hephaestus made armor and weapons. Hephaestus also created the silver arrows of Apollo and Artemis. He even gave Eros his bow and arrows of love. If it was magical or finely made metalwork, Hephaestus was credited with making it in the ancient myths.

DEPENDED ON THE SIZE OF THE CITY-STATE THEY LIVED IN. IN THE SMALLER TOWNS, A BLACKSMITH MIGHT MAKE SWORDS, PLOWS, AXES, AND OTHER TOOLS. IN A LARGER CITY, HE WOULD SPECIALIZE IN MAKING JUST ONE PRODUCT.

Ancient Greeks believed Hephaestus was also the god of volcanoes. His workshops were said to be located under volcanoes. Helping Hephaestus in his workshops were the mighty Cyclopes. The Cyclopes were the one-eyed giant sons of Gaea, or Mother Earth. The giants were also great blacksmiths. They had helped Zeus defeat the Titans during the war to control the universe. The Cyclopes created Poseidon's trident, Hades's helmet of invisibility, and Zeus's thunderbolts. The Cyclopes stayed on after the war to help Hephaestus build weapons for the gods. The sounds of their hammers could be heard all over Greece.

The Cyclopes towered over humans and had amazing strength. This made them good assistants to Hephaestus. Running a blacksmith's forge was hard work. The god Apollo later killed the Cyclopes and their sons. He wanted revenge for his son Asclepius's murder. Zeus committed the murder with his thunderbolts, but Apollo could not go after Zeus. Instead he killed the makers of the thunderbolts.

VOLCANOES

ANCIENT GREEKS DID NOT UNDERSTAND HOW VOLCANOES WORKED. ONE LEGEND SAID VOLCANOES CAME FROM TYPHON, A HIDEOUS 100-HEADED MONSTER THAT SPEWED LAVA AND FIERY ROCKS FROM ITS MOUTHS. IN THE

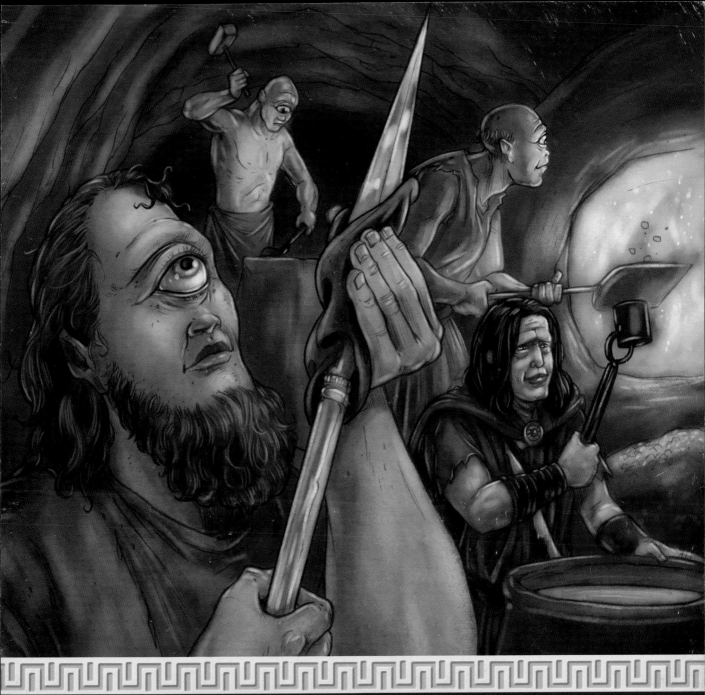

STORY, ZEUS STUCK THE MONSTER TYPHON UNDER MOUNT ETNA TO STOP ITS
MISCHIEF. MOUNT ETNA IS ONE OF THE WORLD'S TALLEST ACTIVE VOLCANOES. IT IS
LOCATED ON THE ISLAND OF SICILY. THE ANCIENT PEOPLE BELIEVED TYPHON WAS
RESPONSIBLE FOR ALL VOLCANIC ERUPTIONS ON EARTH. HEPHAESTUS'S WORKSHOP
WAS ALSO IN MOUNT ETNA. THERE HE HAMMERED MOLTEN ORE.

Hephaestus had three sisters. One was Hebe, the lovely goddess of youth. Eileithyia was another. She was the gentle goddess of childbirth. Then there was Athena. She came into the world with a battle cry.

In one version of Hephaestus's birth, he was there before Athena was born. It began when Zeus swallowed Metis, the first of his many wives and loves. Zeus had heard that their unborn child would one day overthrow him. He swallowed his wife to get rid of the threat. Zeus soon began having pounding headaches. When Zeus could stand it no more he cried for help. Hephaestus ran and got his axe. In one blow he split open his father's forehead. Out jumped Athena as a full-grown warrior.

Hephaestus could not help but like Athena. He just could not figure out how to win her favor. Since both were gods of craftsmen, they shared a common interest. The two gods spent hours in Hephaestus's workshop

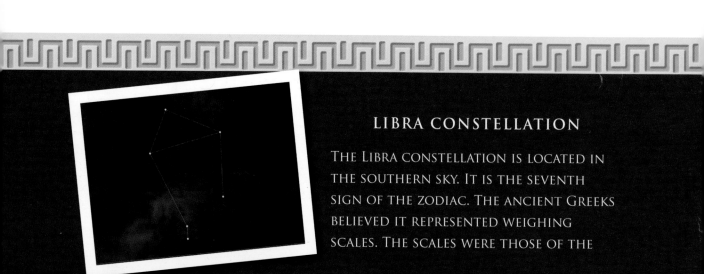

LIBRA CONSTELLATION

THE LIBRA CONSTELLATION IS LOCATED IN THE SOUTHERN SKY. IT IS THE SEVENTH SIGN OF THE ZODIAC. THE ANCIENT GREEKS BELIEVED IT REPRESENTED WEIGHING SCALES. THE SCALES WERE THOSE OF THE

perfecting their skills. Hephaestus even taught Athena how to work the forge. This was the furnace he used to heat up metal. When Hephaestus let Athena know of his love for her, she rejected him. He was heartbroken. Hephaestus decided that he would win the hand of one even more beautiful than Athena. He set his sights on Aphrodite.

GODDESS OF JUSTICE, ASTRAEA. SHE WAS A DAUGHTER OF ZEUS. WHEN SHE LEFT EARTH, ZEUS PLACED HER IN THE SKY AS THE CONSTELLATION VIRGO. HE THEN PLACED ASTRAEA'S SCALES BESIDE HER. ANCIENT GREEKS BELIEVED THAT HEPHAESTUS CREATED THE SCALES AND WAS THEIR PROTECTOR.

Hephaestus soon saw his next opportunity. Like all of the gods on Mount Olympus he admired the goddess Aphrodite. It was hard not to respond to her charms. Aphrodite was, after all, the goddess of love and beauty. Hephaestus was sure she would never notice him. He felt she could never love someone as ugly as him. His luck was soon to change, however.

Hephaestus never forgot the cruel treatment he received from his mother Hera. As a master craftsman he used his skills to create a beautiful golden throne. Hephaestus gave it to Hera as a gift. Unable to resist, Hera accepted the magnificent throne. But as soon as Hera sat on the throne she was trapped. None of the other gods could figure out how to release her. When they asked Hephaestus to free Hera, he refused. Then Dionysus, the god of wine, got Hephaestus drunk. And Hephaestus finally agreed to free Hera. Hephaestus drove a hard bargain though. He would only do so if Hera promised him Aphrodite as his wife. The deal was sealed and the two were married.

Hephaestus wanted to make his wife happy. He used his skill to create a girdle for her. A girdle is a piece of women's clothing that is worn around the waist and chest. It was made of the finest gold. Hephaestus wove magic into the girdle's design. It was to be his greatest gift. But the girdle's magic worked too well. The girdle made all men fall hopelessly in love with its wearer. Combined with Aphrodite's beauty, no one could resist its power. Aphrodite loved her gift and used it to trap all sorts of gods and men, including Hephaestus's brother Ares.

Aphrodite did not like the lame and ugly Hephaestus. She much preferred his more handsome brother Ares. So Aphrodite and Ares began to meet in secret. They were sure they could keep Hephaestus in the dark about their affair. But secrets did not last long on Mount Olympus. Soon Hephaestus found out. Sad and angry, he set a trap for them. Hephaestus created a magical net. It was made of nearly invisible bronze links. One night

HARMONIA'S NECKLACE

HEPHAESTUS WAS NOT ALWAYS KIND IN HIS GIFT GIVING. HEPHAESTUS HELD A GRUDGE AGAINST ARES AND APHRODITE FOR BETRAYING HIM. HEPHAESTUS WAS STILL ANGRY OVER THEIR AFFAIR.

as Ares and Aphrodite slept, Hephaestus cast his net over them. Hephaestus then brought all the gods to judge the trapped pair. He hoped the embarrassment would cause Ares to end the affair. In the end the other gods could not blame Ares. After all, who could resist Aphrodite? Hephaestus went on to have other loves and many children, but none were as dear to his heart as Aphrodite.

SO HEPHAESTUS GAVE THEIR DAUGHTER HARMONIA A CURSED NECKLACE AS A WEDDING GIFT. THE NECKLACE WOULD ONLY BRING DEATH AND MISFORTUNE TO THOSE WHO POSSESSED IT. IT DOOMED HARMONIA AND HER OFFSPRING TO ENDLESS TRAGEDY.

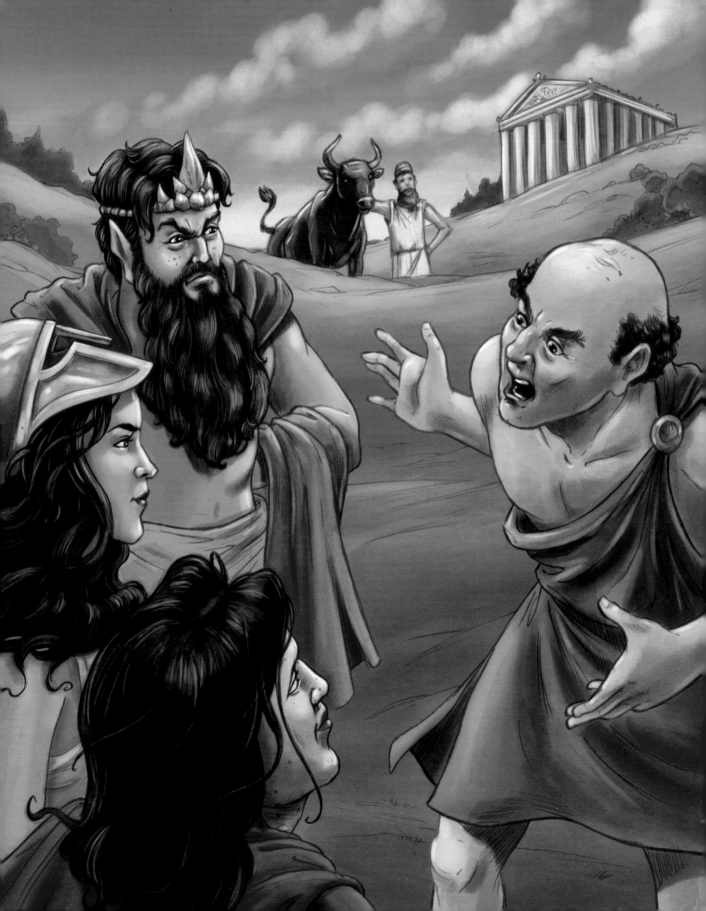

There are many stories that include Hephaestus's inventions. One included his creation of a man. Hephaestus, Athena, and Poseidon were arguing over who was the best craftsman. Momus was asked to judge a contest of skill among the gods. Momus was the god of ridicule and scorn. The gods would later regret choosing him. Each of the three gods presented what they thought was their best invention. Hephaestus created a man. Athena built a house. Poseidon made a bull. Momus was always quick to criticize. So he immediately pointed out the flaws in each god's creation.

He said that Poseidon's bull should have eyes under its horns. This would allow the bull to aim at what it was trying to stab with its horns. To Athena he complained that her house did not have wheels. How else would its owners take it with them when they traveled? Momus finally reached Hephaestus's invention. He wanted to know why they had not put a window in the chest of the man. A window would allow his neighbors to see what he was planning. Zeus was furious and forever banned Momus from Mount Olympus.

Zeus was angry with the men on Earth. The Titan Prometheus had convinced them to trick Zeus. So Zeus came up with a plan to punish them all. Zeus asked Hephaestus to create a beautiful maiden. Hephaestus made her from clay, and the gods gave her many gifts. Aphrodite gave her beauty, Hermes gave her persuasion, and Apollo gave her music. She was named Pandora, which means "all-gifted." When she was complete, the goddess Athena clothed Pandora and breathed life into her. Zeus gave her some gifts as well. He gave Pandora a deep curiosity. Zeus also gave Pandora a sealed box. He told her she was never to open it.

Zeus then sent Pandora to Earth to marry a human. She was happy but she could never forget the sealed box. One day she could not resist the temptation any longer. Pandora decided to take just one peek. What could it hurt? When Pandora opened the box all the evils of the world escaped. Unknown to man these curses would torment all humans. Things like greed, vanity, and jealousy affected how people felt. Pandora managed to close the box right before hope had escaped, too. Zeus had placed hope at the bottom of the box. As long as there was hope, all was not lost. Zeus had succeeded in getting his revenge.

Smart, skilled and generous, Hephaestus had only one downfall—his appearance. Hephaestus had earned the respect of the other gods. They loved his inventions and fabulous gifts. Yet he was never really an equal because he was ugly and lame.

Metalworkers and blacksmiths worshipped Hephaestus. His temples were located all over Greece in the manufacturing and industrial centers. Hephaestus had several feasts and festivals held in his honor. During the Chalceia festival in Athens, his worshippers came together to celebrate his invention of bronze working.

The Roman god Vulcan was similar to Hephaestus. Vulcan was also the god of fire. However, Vulcan was associated with the damaging side of fire. His worshippers prayed to him to prevent fires. Vulcan began to take on the qualities of Hephaestus when Rome invaded Greece. Hephaestus may have had a minor role in the Greek myths, but the god of fire was important to the blacksmiths, craftsmen, and metalworkers of the ancient world.

TEMPLE OF HEPHAESTUS

IN 449 BC A BEAUTIFUL TEMPLE WAS BEGUN OVERLOOKING THE AGORA IN ATHENS. THE AGORA WAS THE MARKETPLACE AND CIVIC CENTER. IT WAS ONE OF THE MOST IMPORTANT PARTS OF THE

ANCIENT CITY. IT WAS BUILT TO HONOR HEPHAESTUS. THE TEMPLE'S DOMINANT
POSITION IN THE CITY SHOWS HOW IMPORTANT HEPHAESTUS WAS AS THE GOD
OF CRAFTSMEN. THE TEMPLE OF HEPHAESTUS IS A BEAUTIFULLY PRESERVED
EXAMPLE OF ANCIENT GREEK ARCHITECTURE.

PRINCIPAL GODS OF GREEK MYTHOLOGY –
A FAMILY TREE

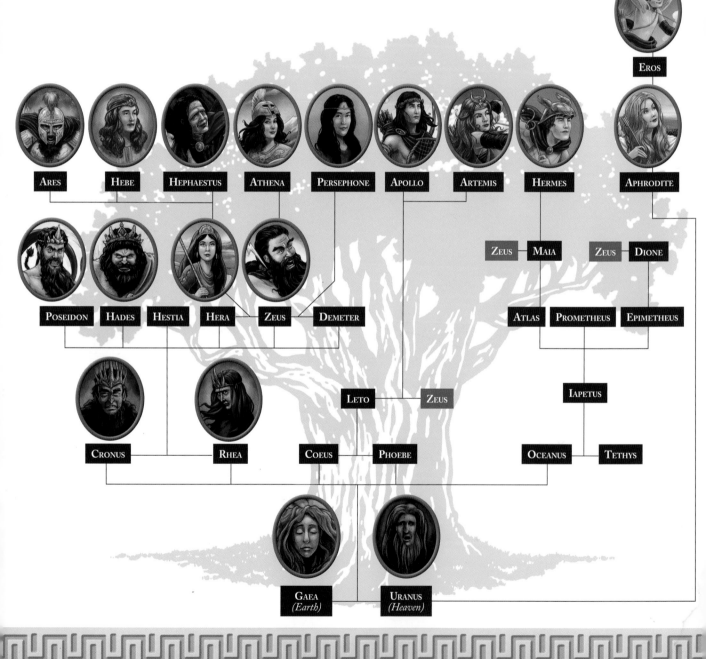

EROS

ARES   HEBE   HEPHAESTUS   ATHENA   PERSEPHONE   APOLLO   ARTEMIS   HERMES   APHRODITE

ZEUS   MAIA   ZEUS   DIONE

POSEIDON   HADES   HESTIA   HERA   ZEUS   DEMETER   ATLAS   PROMETHEUS   EPIMETHEUS

LETO   ZEUS   IAPETUS

CRONUS   RHEA   COEUS   PHOEBE   OCEANUS   TETHYS

GAEA
(Earth)   URANUS
(Heaven)

THE ROMAN GODS

A s the Roman Empire expanded by conquering new lands the Romans often took on aspects of the customs and beliefs of the people they conquered. From the ancient Greeks they took their arts and sciences. They also adopted many of their gods and the myths that went with them into their religious beliefs. While the names were changed, the stories and legends found a new home.

ZEUS: *Jupiter*
King of the Gods, God of Sky and Storms
Symbols: *Eagle and Thunderbolt*

HERA: *Juno*
Queen of the Gods, Goddess of Marriage
Symbols: *Peacock, Cow, and Crow*

POSEIDON: *Neptune*
God of the Sea and Earthquakes
Symbols: *Trident, Horse, and Dolphin*

HADES: *Pluto*
God of the Underworld
Symbols: *Helmet, Metals, and Jewels*

ATHENA: *Minerva*
Goddess of Wisdom, War, and Crafts
Symbols: *Owl, Shield, and Olive Branch*

ARES: *Mars*
God of War
Symbols: *Vulture and Dog*

ARTEMIS: *Diana*
Goddess of Hunting and Protector of Animals
Symbols: *Stag and Moon*

APOLLO: *Apollo*
God of the Sun, Healing, Music, and Poetry
Symbols: *Laurel, Lyre, Bow, and Raven*

HEPHAESTUS: *Vulcan*
God of Fire, Metalwork, and Building
Symbols: *Fire, Hammer, and Donkey*

APHRODITE: *Venus*
Goddess of Love and Beauty
Symbols: *Dove, Sparrow, Swan, and Myrtle*

EROS: *Cupid*
God of Love
Symbols: *Quiver and Arrows*

HERMES: *Mercury*
God of Travels and Trade
Symbols: *Staff, Winged Sandals, and Helmet*

FURTHER INFORMATION

Books

Napoli, Donna Jo. *Treasury of Greek Mythology: Classic Stories of Gods, Goddesses, Heroes & Monsters*. Washington, DC: National Geographic Society, 2011.

Reusser, Kayleen. *Hephaestus*. Hockessin, DE: Mitchell Lane Publishers, 2010.

Turnbull, Ann. *Greek Myths*. Somerville, MA: Candlewick Press, 2011.

Web Sites

Visit our Web site for links about Hephaestus: **childsworld.com/links**

Note to Parents, Teachers, and Librarians: We routinely verify our Web links to make sure they are safe and active sites. So encourage your readers to check them out!

INDEX

Rockwell Media Center
Whittlesey Drive
Bethel, CT 06801